You
Should
Know
About
World
Religions

Charlene Altemose, MSC

Liguori
ONE LIGUORI DRIVE
LIGUORI MO 63057-9999

Imprimi Potest:
Richard Thibodeau, C.Ss.R.
Provincial, Denver Province
The Redemptorists

Imprimatur:
Most Reverend Robert J. Hermann
Auxiliary Bishop, Archdiocese of St. Louis

ISBN 0-7648-1254-8
Library of Congress Catalog Card Number: 2004115015

© 2005, Charlene Altemose, MSC
Printed in the United States of America
05 06 07 08 09 5 4 3 2 1

All rights reserved. No part of this book may be reproduced,
stored in a retrieval system, or transmitted without the written
permission of Liguori Publications.

Scripture quotations are from the *New Revised Standard Version of
the Bible*, © 1989 by the Division of Christian Education of the
National Council of the Churches of Christ in the USA. Used by
permission. All rights reserved.

Excerpts from *Vatican II: The Basic Sixteen Documents Vatican
Council II*, edited by Austin Flannery, O.P., copyright © 1996, Austin P. Flannery, O.P. are used by permission of the publisher. All
rights reserved.

To order, call 1-800-325-9521
www.liguori.org

Contents

Introduction

Today more than ever we cannot overlook other cultures and religions. *Progress* was the earmark of the twentieth century. *Multiculturalism* is the "in" word of the twenty-first century.

In a matter of hours, a supersonic jet can whisk us to any spot on the globe. Daily the world comes into our homes via newspapers, TV, e-mail, and the Internet. We come in contact with people of all cultures and ways of thinking. We cannot live a detached, monolithic existence. Global awareness and concerns are necessary facts of life.

Although all people share the same fragile human condition, the lifestyles, manners, and cultural ways are as divergent as people themselves. Travel to any country, and differences are evident as soon as you arrive. No longer can we think that our way of doing and thinking is the only way.

In no other sphere of human life are differences more obvious than in the area of religion. Religion continues to have an unparalleled effect on lifestyle, culture and outlook. Religion, as an energizing force, gives life meaning, a value worth living for, and even worth dying for. Religion can cause dissension and division, because people do not understand the rationale behind others' beliefs and practices. Before the cyberspace invasion, most people lived ensconced in a one-world environment, rarely associating with people of other cultures and religions.

I, too, am a product of that world. I was raised in a small Pennsylvania town, Coplay, in which there were two kinds of people: "us Catholics and them Protestants." Although we were not totally isolated from each other, I realized "them Protestants" were different. When I was about seven years old, I spied a Last Supper scene in the kitchen of our Protestant neighbors. How surprised I was to see "our Catholic" Jesus.

I went to Catholic school, had Catholic friends, and joined our Catholic Girl Scout troop. I loved my Catholic faith and ultimately felt called to become a Catholic sister. I joined the Missionary Sisters of the Sacred Heart, the order which taught me in grade and high school. I taught in Catholic schools and earned a degree in theology, the Catholic kind, of course. So, for the first thirty years of my life, I was Catholic through and through

A drastic turning-point in my faith-life occurred when I became a theology professor at Alvernia College, a Catholic institution, in Reading, Pennsylvania. Vatican II encouraged interfaith understanding and because the number of students of different cultures was increasing, I was asked to teach a class in World Religions.

My! What a vista of faiths opened up. I discovered the colorful and unfamiliar ways people express their religious sentiments and faith. The many faces of the sacred unfolded like a spiritual kaleidoscope. How much more cosmic was God than I had ever realized!

The new spiritual horizons broadened my personal faith and approach to God. I thoroughly immersed myself in my new-found world. I took Hebrew lessons at a local synagogue, celebrated Yom Kippur, and sat "Shiva" when a Jewish friend died. I appreciated the reverence of sacred time when I welcomed the Sabbath with my Orthodox Jewish friends. Judaism became more alive and real when I was given a grant to study in Israel.

The Hindu and Buddhist world became real when I went to India, as a Fulbright scholar. The Bhagavad-Gita became part of my spiritual reading.

I co-created the new day the Hindu way as I prayed by the Ganges River at sunrise. I stopped in the streets of Srinagar as the muezzin announced the Islamic noon prayer. I learned the quiet of mental prayer in Zen meditation. The awareness of the present moment impressed me, as I watched a Buddhist monk construct a gravel pathway, stone-by-stone.

I came to understand why people do what they do religiously and so I gained a deep respect and tolerance of all religious expressions. I saw beneath the veneer of external rituals as I recall the words of the fox to the Little Prince: "…what is essential is invisible to the eye" (*The Little Prince,* Antoine de Saint Exupéry).

My Catholic faith is stronger, and open enough to appreciate all faith forms and enter unbiased inter-religious dialogue. I understand that all religions are sincere attempts of the human spirit to answer the dilemmas of life and I greatly respect that.

Have I compromised my faith? Have I become less Catholic? In no way! In fact my spirituality has taken on the literal meaning of the word "catholic" which means "universal." I apply the words of Mahatma Gandhi to my own situation: "I open my windows and doors and allow all cultures and religions to blow about freely, but I do not get swept off my feet by any."

With this cosmopolitan frame of mind, I gladly share my insights. I realize that not everyone has had my varied spiritual opportunities. But it is my burning desire to impart a deeper understanding of other faiths, paraphrasing the Scotch poet Burns' words: "Oh, what giftie the good God gie us, to see other religions as they see themselves" (see *To A Louse*, by Robert Burns).

What You Should Know About World Religions, invites you to embark on a journey into other faiths. We travel through the seven main world religions and experience that particular faith as do the believers. We consider the religions of the world in an objective way, touch upon their history, rituals, beliefs, and customs. After we explore each world religion, we consider what Catholics can learn from each.

In Part One, we explore the vital role which faith plays in the world, and how religion affects every aspect of life. We examine the elements common to all religions, a necessary ingredient toward interfaith understanding. Part One also explains the Eastern and Western world views.

In Part Two we visit the Far East: India, China, and Japan, where Hinduism, Buddhism, Confucianism/Taoism, and Shinto are rooted and where the Eastern world view dominates. We enter the lives and faith of the believers and try to see reality and the sacred as they do.

In Part Three we journey to the Middle East, the Mediterranean lands where we meet Abraham, the father of the monotheistic religions—Judaism, Christianity, and Islam. These religions believe in one God with whom one can establish a personal relationship. Although each religion shares the same spiritual father, they differ in their interpretations, practices, and theology.

Part Four examines the theological breakthroughs of Vatican II and the efforts of Pope John Paul II toward interfaith understanding. The chapter concludes with practical ways that people of differing faiths can foster interreligious dialogue, communication, and respect.

If, through this work, you become more compassionate to the ways people worship and pray, if you learn the value of being open to other ways of thinking, if you appreciate your own religious heritage more and are determined to practice it with greater fervor, and if you resolve to be a harbinger of peace and understanding among people of all religious persuasions, then *What You Should Know About World Religions* has served its purpose well. We can look forward to a world in which people of all religions live in harmony, tolerance, and mutual respect.

PART 1

Origins and Overview of World Religions

We are about to embark on a marvelous journey, which takes us from the depths of the human heart to the heights of the divine via the living religions of the world. As we begin our odyssey into the world's religions, let us come with openness that is attuned to the many voices crying out to the divine.

In our journey into this sacred world, we must be free of our notions and stereotypes of ways humans reach out to God. If we approach other religions with wonder, respect, and empathy, we may be able to see them as they see themselves. If we try to put on their faith-view, and experience the divine as they do, we can better understand the rationale behind their beliefs—why they do what they do—even though we cannot relate to or agree with their notions. As we explore the world's religions, may our own faith commitment be deepened, enlarged, and enriched.

Human Experience and Religious Aspirations

On this journey we will delve into the myriad ways peoples answer the mysteries of life and how they communicate with God. We begin our odyssey within ourselves and our human experience, where religious aspirations originate.

Human Experience

World View

Each of us is born in time, of certain parents, and in a particular place. Our parents give us life, food, and shelter. They clothe and nurture us in our growing-up years. From them we learn how to live and act. We absorb attitudes and perceptions about the world around us. Our natural life, parents, and upbringing provide us with our initial experience of living. This is our "world view."

Cultural Heritage

No one is born into an empty world. Nature equips us with amenities which help us grow and develop. From people around us, we learn how to behave, speak, eat, and live a certain way. We learn how to conduct ourselves, what is appropriate and what is not, and how to distinguish right from wrong. The people we associate with, the age in which we live, and the environment in which we grow, influence our whole life. This overall learned way of living and acting is our "cultural heritage."

Personal Uniqueness

We are also endowed with natural gifts which no one else possesses. We are "one of a kind," no matter what scientists say about cloning. As God's unique creation with our specific temperament, talents, gifts, and tendencies, we each have a specific role in this world which no one else can fill.

Our parentage, environment, nationality, language, culture, and individuality are nature's gifts to us. Each one born into this world possesses these natural endowments to a greater or lesser degree. All humans experience the same needs, hopes, dreams, and joys, as well as sorrows and death. We are all alike in our fundamental humanity and basic needs. It is the universal "human condition."

Origins of Religion

From the dawn of civilization, people realized there were some aspects of life over which humans had no control—the weather, rhythm of the seasons, day and night, and other natural occurrences. People also questioned the suffering, pain, and death which all experience.

These are baffling mysteries of life, beyond the scope of human understanding. We soon realize we are limited and do not have control over everything. Many questions about life remain above human understanding.

From earliest times, people believed there was some sacred "Power" greater than themselves which commanded nature and controlled life's mysteries. Life is purposeful when it is connected with the sacred. At times this "Power" assumed human characteristics and was given a name. At other times, as is the case with Judaism, Christianity, and Islam, the "Power" revealed its nature and identity.

Humans thought that they could influence this unseen power by establishing a friendly relationship with it. They reasoned that life was more fulfilling when they lived in friendship and accord with this "power greater than human understanding." A relationship with the divine gave answers to life's baffling questions, especially regarding death and the afterlife. Throughout the ages people have related to the divine by prayer, rituals, and offerings. People discovered that when they bonded in community and utilized meaningful ways to communicate with the sacred, they experienced peace and serenity.

Origins of Religion

As people settled in different parts of the world and had their unique world views and culture, they devised creative ways to relate to the divine and developed various answers to life's baffling mysteries. This is generally how religions started.

The Elements and Purpose of Religion

Although the world religions may differ in externals, each religion possesses characteristics in common with others. Religions have more similarities than differences, for each one attempts to link with the mystery of the sacred and unknown.

The Elements of Religion

Faith

Each religion began in time. Just as a growing, living organism changes and evolves into different forms as time goes on, so too does religion. The living religions have been kept alive by believers who pass the faith on to succeeding generations. When a religion is not passed on, the religion dies out or it merges with another.

Each religion exists because people acknowledged and have been aware of a higher sacred power. Whether as a universal power, cosmic force, or a personal god, the object of religion has always been belief in the transcendent. The transcendent is something outside the scope of human experience. It is not bound by our human limitations.

Most religions began when people joined together to affirm their beliefs. Religion provides a sense of belonging to believers. People felt more power in togetherness with others than alone. No religion ever thrives outside of community. Within a religion, however, the level of commitment ranges from ardent and fanatic adherents to those who only nominally belong to a religion.

Community

The Purpose of Religion

Most religions put into human terms what is believed about the spiritual through doctrines, creeds, and theology. People make the sacred understandable through stories and myths which explain spiritual truths in human analogies. Each religion can be identified with certain symbols or signs which convey a deeper meaning and point to a spiritual reality or truth. Some religions believe their sacred writings are revealed and are inspired.

Stories of Belief

To live nobly and to bring goodness into the world is what religions hope to accomplish. Moral codes of conduct direct the followers how to live in accordance with the mandates of their religion. A religion usually determines what is good and permissible or what is evil and prohibitive. Who are we? Why are we here? What is our destiny? Each religion addresses the problems of the human condition and provides remedies for a good life.

Code of Behavior

Through prayer, worship, and ritual, which takes many forms, believers make contact with the divine. Almost every human act and things people use in life have been used in religious rituals.

Ritual

Western and Eastern World Views

As we explore the religions of the world we find that, although they have common elements, there are stark differences in how people view the world and their concept of the sacred. For our purposes here, we distinguish between two divergent world views—the Western and the Eastern world views.

Western World View

Linear View of Reality

Most of us who read this book, come from the "Western world view." It is a linear approach to reality. Life begins at a certain time, we live one life for a span of years and then die. Our souls are immortal and our spirit continues to exist in eternity. We believe we are created by God who desires a relationship of love with us. If we lead a good life we will spend an eternity of happiness in heaven.

In this Western world view, human life is dependent on God as Creator who revealed his being. The laws of life provide our moral basis and govern our relation to God, others, and ourselves. The religions of Christians, Jews, and Muslims share this Western world view.

Eastern World View

Cyclic View of Reality

The Eastern world view is a cyclic view of reality. People witnessed the regularity of seasons and concluded that human life flows on and on like nature's rhythms. Life seemed a never-ending spiral with the "Ultimate Reality" and source of all being at the core.

Life and reality, in this Oriental mind-set and cyclic view of reality, continues through many lives and rebirths. People enter life at a certain point in the spiral according to their merits in a previous life. Life continues and after death one enters the flow of life, either lower or higher on the evolutionary scale, depending on one's moral merits or failures of one's former life.

Reincarnation

The final goal is to merge and become one with the ultimate center of reality. To lose one's identity in the world and become one's true self united with the absolute constitutes a person's life destiny. But first one needs to peel away layers of ignorance, imperfections, and evil which prevent one from becoming one's "true self." It cannot be accomplished in a single lifetime, so one needs many rebirths or reincarnations to achieve unity with the ultimate.

Union With the Ultimate

Religions of the East

The Eastern world view dominates the religions of the East, which is the subject of part two. In particular, we will consider the religious traditions from India, China, and Japan.

Hinduism—Religion of India

Religion is everywhere in India. It is a kaleidoscope of images: temples, scantily-clad holy men squatting crossed-legged, kiosks laden with gaudy gods, processions, pilgrims bathing in the sacred river, gurus, and swamis. All are part of the tapestry of India's religion. What unites this melange is the world view and religious faith of Hinduism.

Origins of Hinduism

Hinduism is unique among the world religions. It evolved gradually and has no founder, set rules, or uniform rituals. Hinduism is a religion in which all practice their religion as the spirit moves them. The heart of the

Heart of
Hinduism

Hindu faith lies in the Eastern world view, or cyclic pattern of existence.

Vedas   From earliest recorded history, people and civilizations settled along earth's river systems. The Indus and Ganges rivers became home for Aryans and native Dravidians who interpreted the world and the mysteries of life according to their experience and observation. Because these peoples experienced drought, floods, and other powers of nature, water became a sacred symbol and natural forces were worshiped as gods.

To assuage the unseen powers, people composed hymns of praise and chants to the gods. These *Vedas,* India's oldest sacred literature, were first handed on orally and later written in Sanskrit.

Upanishads   As time went on, people began questioning their beliefs and sought explanations which scholars and philosophers explained in volumes of the *Upanishads,* teachings about truth and reality. This unique outlook blossomed, over thousands of years, into the tradition and religion of India, later named Hinduism, because it evolved along the Indus River.

Beliefs of Hinduism

Brahman   Hindus believe that all reality—the ultimate source of being, the universe, all animate and inanimate life— is one. This eternal, infinite, unknowable is Brahman, who is in all, over all, beneath all, and through all. All that exists shares the identical essence. All is Brahman. This concept transcends human understanding, but will be comprehended only when one becomes the "eternal self," or *Atman.*

In the cyclic pattern of existence, people are born, live, die, and are reborn into another life either in a higher or lower form depending on their merits in a previous life. Each is created and reborn many times because one cannot attain this perfection in one lifetime. Hindus believe they need many lives to escape rebirth and merge into Brahman. The goal of life is to escape the cycle of rebirths and to merge into the one absolute reality.

Karma

One enters life at a certain point according to the way one lived in the last life. Every action, every moment stores up either helpful or harmful effects. This is the law of karma. If one accumulates good karma, in the next life one will come back on a higher plane. If one amasses bad karma, the next life will be lower. Like the natural law, what you reap, you sow. Each one is morally responsible for every action. If one's present lot brings hardships and suffering, it is due to past evil deeds. The goal of life is to accumulate as much good karma as one can, so that one's next life is on a higher plane.

Dharma

One gains good karma by living according to one's *dharma*—duty and responsibilities—which depends on one's caste, age, and role in life. What is expected in one's specific role in life is one's *dharma*. This changes and is different in different situations. If one lives *dharma* faithfully, one reaps good karma and in the next life can be born into a higher caste.

Life Stages

Each stage of life brings with it corresponding duties and responsibilities, which change with age. The first stage of moral responsibility is the role of student. A student has responsibilities to study, learn, work hard, and prepare for a living.

When one marries and provides for a family, the stage of householder brings additional and different responsibilities. After one has raised a family, one takes life easier which gives more time for reflection, prayer, and meditation. These stages are the normal pattern of life. To hurry up the process of rebirth and amass more good karma, one can give up one's earthly possessions and live as a *sannyasi,* a wandering Hindu holy person.

Castes From earliest times, people realized the inequality of one's lot in life. People are rich, poor, learned, unlearned, healthy, or ill. Hindus replied to this dilemma with the notion of caste. Four main castes have fashioned and determined India's social status and occupation.

Brahmins, the most elite caste, are priests, scholars, and teachers. Warriors and administrators compose the Kshatriyas. The Vasihyas are the merchants and artisans. Shudras, are laborers and servants. The untouchable outcasts are the lowest on the scale of humanity.

Caste determines one's affiliations, marriage partner, and social restrictions. One is born into a caste and remains there until death. One's present caste results from past karma. The good or bad karma accumulated in one's life determines whether one returns in the next life in a higher or lower life form.

One can escape the effects of caste by a good life, thus meriting good karma and coming back in the next life in a higher caste. That's why Hindus are content to remain in the condition and caste into which they are born. If one is born a servant, does menial work well, and makes the best of it, that one will be born into a higher caste in the next life.

Although one does not choose caste, how one worships God is open to choice. Just as each person has a definite personality, so one has a distinct way of relating to God. Hinduism recognizes four *yogas* as ways people express their spirituality according to temperament and choice.

People who are activists come to God through good works. Those who reflect on life's meaning relate to God through meditation and prayer. A common avenue to God is by devotion and love. These ways are the ordinary spiritual paths. The *yoga* is the one who renounces the world through discipline and bodily asceticism.

Yoga

Many Gods of Hinduism

Hinduism boasts myriads of gods and goddesses depicted with distinct features and symbols. Three gods, Brahma, Vishnu, and Shiva make up what is sometimes called the "Hindu Trinity." Other popular gods include: Ganesh, the elephant god, Hanuman, the monkey god, and Lakshmi, goddess of wealth. Some gods come to earth as "avatars" (incarnations of gods), such as Krishna and Rama. Hindus insist that they do not worship the image, but the trait the god symbolizes.

Brahma, Vishnu, Shiva

The Mahabharata and the Ramayana, classic stories of the escapades and adventures of the gods, are popular features in movies and drama. The most popular and well-known story is the "Bhagavad-Gita"—The Song of the Lord, the "Hindu Bible." It consists of a dialogue between Arjuna, a warrior and Krishna, the incarnation of Vishnu. Its value lies in its high moral quality and tale of a human's moral conflict and responsibility. The story is a classic spiritual work for all religions because all people can relate to the moral conflicts we face in life, and the wish to do the right thing. We are all dependent on a

Bhagavad-Gita

higher power no matter how we name it. Moral dilemmas occur in everyone's life and we need to make right decisions.

Worship, Practices, Rituals

Home
Worship

A Hindu uses all his senses at worship. The customary Hindu worship in a home is called *Puja*. The *Puja* place is either a nook or an entire room. On the altar, images of the god or gods are prominently displayed as well as flowers, food, and offerings for the god. Incense sticks emit a pleasant scent.

Before performing *Puja*, a Hindu takes off his shoes, washes his body, and in clean clothes, appears before the god. Sitting on the floor lower than the god out of respect, he greets the god with *Namaste!* It means, "the god in me greets the god in you." He then chants the sacred sound "Om" in guttural and prolonged tones.

The worshiper washes the god with milk and clarified butter and dresses it in royal colors. After placing the god back in its niche, the worshiper reflects and prays and waves the incense stick back and forth. Passages may be read from the Bhagavad-Gita or the Vedas. Finally, one offers fresh fruit and food to the god. The worshiper bows and partakes of the food as a symbol of sharing. Devout Hindus perform this *Puja* daily.

Temple
Worship

Hindu temples dot the countryside and dominate village skylines. Some are ornately gilded and display the OM symbol which resembles the numeral three and a "s" with a marking above it. Other temples are simple in appearance. People go to a temple to ask the Brahmin priest to pray to the god and offer gifts for a special intention. Most temples are dedicated to a specific god or gods and are honored with gala festivals by devotees.

Pilgrims throng to hundreds of temples, sacred rivers, and sacred sites scattered throughout India. At Benares (Varanasi), India's holiest city, people flock to the Ganges River, bathe in its waters and pray that they die there so their ashes can be strewn in the sacred waters. People assemble at sunrise to co-create the new day with the creator. Hindus believe each new day is a gift from the gods and they hail the new day by washing and praying in the sacred waters.

Pilgrims sit in meditation by the Ganges on platforms called *ghats.* They ring bells; splatter themselves with the holy waters and chant prayers. Hindus often wear a red mark on the forehead, as a sign of their devotion.

Diwali is the Hindu new year, or the Festival of Lights. It is celebrated in October. Business accounts are settled and a new ledger is opened for the start of the fiscal year. People parade, dance, and sing while waving lanterns, candles, and lamps to ward off evil and for good luck. The city is ablaze with lights strung over doorways as they pray to Lakshmi, the goddess of wealth, to bless them with prosperity and a good livelihood.

The four arms of the Lakshmi symbolizes her generosity, acceptance, and welcome. She is a popular goddess but, since she has no temple of her own, her good luck image is included in many temples and decorates the entrance to people's homes. The *Diwali* holiday closes with gigantic fireworks and with sirens blaring.

Holi, celebrated at the spring full moon, ranks as a universal Hindu festival. Originally an agricultural feast, *Holi* heralds spring and honors fertility. Merriment dominates and *Holi* is a popular, frivolous time.

Celebrations of Life Cycles

Early Years   Hindus celebrate life's stepping stones at home, in a temple, or by a river. When a child is still young, the parents, at sunrise, offer the child to the god of creation and pray for a good life. A child's first step, first tooth, haircut, solid food, ear piercing, and other significant events, are marked with rituals of thanksgiving and prayer.

When a young boy, especially of the priestly caste, reaches his teens, he takes on religious responsibilities by initiation with a sacred thread which he wears the rest of his life.

Marriages   Hindus believe in arranged marriages, that is, parents choose their children's spouses, usually of the same caste. The couple does not meet until the wedding day, for Hindus believe one does not fall in love, but that love develops after marriage. Hindus marry not just a person, but marry into a family. The extended family plays an important role in Hindu relationships.

The wedding ceremony itself is elaborate and festive. Whole villages participate in the gala for many days. The bride's father presents his daughter to the groom along with a specified dowry. The bride and groom, dressed in bright colors and bedecked with numerous strands of beads and tassels, walk around a sacred fire and pledge their lives to each other.

Death   Because one hopes to achieve a rapid transition to the next life, Hindus cremate a person soon after death to get rid of all remains of earthly life, so the person can enter the next life unhindered. A Hindu's most sacred desire is to be cremated by the Ganges and have one's ashes strewn in the sacred waters. As the litter is set on the cremation *ghat,* the oldest son circles the pyre reciting prayers. As the body is drenched with *ghee*, a refined butter, the fire is lit. The family mourners stand in silent grief until the skull is split open by the fire's heat, a sign that the soul is released from its former life and ready to be reborn.

Spiritual Insights and Values
- Awareness and respect for silence and meditation.
- A nonviolent attitude.
- Reverence for all life, including animals.
- Respect and tolerance for all forms of worship.

Buddhism—Religion of the Enlightened One

Hinduism solved the mysteries of life by belief in one Brahman. Buddha upheld belief in reincarnation and final liberation called Nirvana. He rejected the belief that one becomes absorbed into Brahman. He rejected the Hindu gods, elaborate temple rituals, the caste system, and extreme asceticism. An exceptional human being, Siddhartha Gautama, shared the Eastern world view of reincarnation, but answered the dilemmas of life more simply. One can attain Nirvana or liberation through one's efforts and bypass many rebirths.

The Origins of Buddhism

Unlike Hinduism which had no founder, Buddhism began with Siddhartha Gautama who was born about 560 BC into the warrior caste, amid luxury and splendor, shielded from life's ills and hardships. He soon grew weary of his privileged lifestyle and set out to explore the real world.

Siddhartha Gautama

He met a sick person, an old person, and a dead person, which disheartened him. He then met a *sannyasi,* a holy man who had renounced all riches, but who radiated peace and happiness. These four encounters led Siddhartha to renounce his family and wealth and live as a wandering ascetic in search of enlightenment. After years of fasting he became emaciated and weak. He sought enlightenment under a tree until he could find contentment and peace. On the seventh day he experienced enlightenment and set out to share this insight with five friends. In the Deer Park Sermon he explained his new-found formula for enlightenment—the "Middle Way."

Siddhartha, the Buddha or the "Enlightened One," traveled with his companions throughout India, teaching the way to enlightenment expressed as the Four Noble Truths and the Eight-fold Path. During the rainy season, they settled in one spot and thus began Buddhism's monasticism, the *Sangha.* Because Buddha believed that the spiritual life can be most fully achieved with the support of others, the monastic community became part of the Buddhist way of life. Buddha continued preaching until 480 BC. At age eighty, he peacefully entered Nirvana. Buddha was never considered a god, but people reverenced him by imitating his virtues. After his death, Buddhism split into two branches—Theravada Buddhism (The Lesser Vehicle), for monks, and Mahayana Buddhism (Greater Vehicle), where enlightenment could be achieved by anyone.

Theravada
Buddhism

Theravada Buddhism, promoting the monastic lifestyle, continued Buddha's legacy in southeast Asia. The monks preached the way of the Buddha, compiled his teachings, and wrote Buddha's sayings onto palm leaves preserved in wicker baskets. Thus the sacred writings of Theravada Buddhism were called "the Three Baskets" and stress the Middle Way, monastic rules, and the *sangha* (community).

Mahayana Buddhism, the "Greater Vehicle" taught that ordinary people can achieve enlightenment. This Buddhism spread into China, Korea, and Japan which subsequently spawned a variety of sects in those countries. A redeemer-like concept evolved , the Boddhissatva. A Boddhissatva was a person who postponed Nirvana to help others attain it.

Mahayana Buddhism

The Buddhism of Nepal and Tibet developed its own system of monastic and esoteric practices. Chanting, prayer wheels, and prayer flags, which wave in the mountain breeze, activate all the prayers. Tibetan Buddhism stressed the monastic element and at times most of the male population were lamas or monks. The current Dalai Lama, Tibet's fourteenth spiritual and civil leader, is believed to be the reincarnation of his predecessor. He was chosen at the death of the thirteenth Dalai Lama by auspicious signs.

Tibetan Buddhism— Lamaism

The Middle Way
Buddha came to understand life's stark realities through the Four Noble Truths.

The Four Noble Truths

1. Life in this world involves suffering.
2. Suffering results from selfish cravings and desires.
3. Suffering will cease once one abolishes cravings, so finally one can be totally free.
4. The way to liberation lies in following the Middle Way.

The Eight-fold Path provides a model for completeness and wholeness. It encompasses all that helps one be a well-rounded personality and provides proper guidelines to accomplish one's goals. Perfection lies in one's mind-set, thought control, and practice of moderation.

1. Right understanding helps one distinguish between the wholesome and unwholesome.
2. Right motives provide the reasoning behind one's acts.
3. Right mindfulness and awareness allows one to focus on the present moment.
4. Right speech allows one to say the proper thing.
5. Right action promotes proper behavior which redounds to one's goodness.
6. Right livelihood provides one with work suited to one's abilities.
7. Right effort encourages one to accomplish goals through perseverance and drive.
8. Right concentration teaches that perfect peace comes through contemplation and meditation.

Buddha affirmed that when one perfectly follows this formula and procedure, one enters Nirvana. Like extinguishing the flame of a candle, one becomes totally selfless and free through Nirvana, the ultimate aim and crux of Buddhism.

Contemplation

Buddhism lacks elaborate rituals. Buddhist worship is essentially stillness and quietude performed by individuals at prayer or in contemplation of a Buddha image. The most ceremonious Buddhist ritual may be when a young man enters the monastery.

Buddhism in China

Around the first century AD, a Mahayana Buddhist came to China and translated Buddha's teaching into Chinese. This appealed to the Chinese because Mahayana Buddhism promised salvation to ordinary lay people without needing to become a monk in the *Sangha*. This form of Buddhism did not conflict with other Chinese practices because it easily blended the yin and yang notion to Taoist meditation and Confucian ethics. It's common to live according to Confucius' teaching, pray the Taoist way, and be buried like a Buddhist.

The memory of Buddha is kept alive by Chinese-style memorials called pagodas. These usually have eight sides to recall Buddha's Eight-fold Path and levels of upturned roofs to symbolize one's spiritual journey.

The Chinese image of Buddha has a rounded head. His right hand is raised, with the thumb and forefinger in a circle and three fingers straight, in the Buddha sign of blessing.

The overweight "laughing Buddha" with Chinese features is Maitreya, the loving Buddha who will return to earth as the last Buddha. The image is a favorite with children who swarm around and sit on his lap.

Spiritual Insights and Values
- Moral integrity and aiming toward moral perfection.
- Awareness of the present moment.
- Stillness through interior silence.

Religions of China—
Confucianism and Taoism

We look again at China, which for thousands of years remained isolated from the rest of the world, hemmed in by mountains, deserts, and seas. China endures as an ancient civilization with its unique language and interpretation of life's mysteries.

Our common notion that religion involves a "god" does not apply to China. While India's people looked inward, and stressed the spiritual aspect of existence, the Chinese looked around and developed world-oriented beliefs.

Ancient Chinese Cosmology

The Spirit World   In prehistoric times, the Chinese noted the order and rhythm of the heavenly bodies and seasons. Chinese believed that the unseen spirit world along with the natural world formed a unity. The whole purpose of life was to keep harmony among the forces of heaven, earth, and people. Because the spirit world had power over good and evil, the Chinese sought to placate the spirit gods by offering sacrifices.

Rulers and Family Ties   The Chinese revered the rulers as heavenly powers. Royal dynasties ruled China until 1912 when China became a republic. The closely-knit Chinese believed familial links continued after death. To keep the departed souls at peace, ancestor worship flourished in various forms.

They honored the dead at home with ancestral tablets engraved with names of deceased family members which they placed at a special shrine. They consulted the ancestors for answers to problems, offered foods, and adorned the shrine with flowers. So, before written records, the Chinese answered life's mysteries by revering nature, emperors, and ancestors.

Although the Chinese are not God-centered people, they do value traditions which help them bring harmony into the world. They respect and love each other and keep their ancestors' memory alive. Because China had been cut off from civilization for many years and developed independently, they coped with life's mysteries as they heeded Confucius and Lao-Tzu's advice.

The Chinese developed their world view by observing the balanced order in the world—night and day, cold and heat, women and men, strength and weakness, sorrow and joy, light and dark. Everything seemed governed by one or the other. The secret to happiness was to live with opposites in harmony and peace.

The Yin and Yang

This "yin and yang" principle has affected China's beliefs and lifestyle and guided the Chinese to live peaceably with life's tensions. The yin and yang is portrayed as a circle, the cycle of life, divided with a curved line. Half of the circle is dark with a white dot and half light with a black dot. This stands for the positive and negative energies in the world which do not conflict but exist peaceably side by side. The yin and yang influenced the Chinese in their thinking, values, and beliefs.

Confucianism

Confucius (d. 475 BC) lived at a chaotic time in his country's history and during the time of other great men in the world: Buddha and Socrates. Confucius believed that harmony would exist if people observed the traditions of their ancestors. He had studied the classics— history, poetry, rites, music, annals, and the *Book of*

Confucius

Changes—and came to appreciate the "good old days." He traveled from town to town and propagated the teachings of the ancients and instilled in all who heard him a desire for the goodness and integrity of times past.

He believed that a proper social order comes about if all people follow certain rules of human conduct.

Writings on Confucianism Confucianism, not considered a religion in the ordinary sense, preaches a moral goodness common to most religions. After his death, temples were erected to Confucius and his sayings engraved on tablets. Mencius kept alive his teachings by compiling the *Analects* which are the sayings of Confucius. *The Great Learning* served as a classic textbook for students. *The Doctrine of the Mean* explained how human nature is linked to the moral order of the universe. Confucius' thoughts and philosophy are recorded in the *Book of Mencius.* Gradually the message of Confucius became the standard for government positions. When the Communists took over in 1949, Confucius' teachings and books were destroyed. Today, the Confucian spirit thrives on the island of Taiwan, where the nationalists fled in 1949.

Spiritual Insights and Values

- An acceptance of one's social role and obligations to bring about peace and justice.
- Fidelity to moral principles is a necessity for proper decorum and lifestyle.

Taoism

Lao-Tzu Taoism was developed around the same time as Confucius by Lao-Tzu. Because we know so little about his life, people wonder whether his life is legendary. Like Confucius, Lao-Tzu, was a scholar concerned about the turmoil in his country. Disgusted, he decided to leave the country and seek solitude in Tibet. As he was leaving, the gatekeeper would not let him go until he wrote down his beliefs and teachings. After several days Lao-Tzu handed the guard a slim volume named the *Tao-Te Ching*.

While Confucius believed that human relationships were at the heart of the well-being of society, Lao-Tzu believed peaceful harmony lay within the world and nature. Called *Tao*, it is peace, harmony, and a patient acceptance of all that is. Although the notion of *Tao* seems complex, it reflects a simplicity and harmony.

Tao has no sound and does not change; it is the source and root of the universe and flows everywhere. All of life depends on *Tao*. It orders all and nurtures all, as the ultimate basis of all life. It is impersonal and not even named. It is *Tao*—the way. The whole purpose of life is to live in harmony with *Tao,* to allow things to go the natural way as they were meant to go. It is a simple message, but difficult for the Western mind to comprehend.

Tao helps us cut down friction and conflict by accepting all that happens with equanimity. So *Tao* teaches us to conserve and manage our energy in our daily tasks. True mastery is gained by letting go.

Spiritual Insights and Values

- Accept all in life as God's will and accept all as coming from God's goodness.
- Try to see both sides of a situation.
- Do the best we can do at the proper moment and allow nature to take its course.

Religion of Japan—Shinto

We next travel to Nippon or Japan, the Land of the Rising Sun. Thousands of islands are dotted with beautiful greenery, lakes, waterfalls, and volcanoes. The Japanese, aware of the beauties of nature and the spirit world, explained life's mysteries and religious questions through their way of life—Shinto.

Origins of Shinto

Kami

From earliest days, the Japanese were keenly aware of impersonal forces of nature, the places or things which control the world. They called these mysterious forces which influence all aspects of life *Kami. Kami* are present everywhere in nature, events, and ancestors. Anything animate or inanimate exuding power and inspiring awe is *Kami*. Their inherent power can bring havoc or blessing, so worshipers assuage them through prayers and offerings. The belief in *Kami* is a way of life and basis of the native Japanese religion, Shinto.

Creation Mythology

Shinto evolved from experiences and observation of nature which inspire awe and wonder. With no founder, scriptures, ethical laws, creeds, dogmas, or stipulated ceremonies, Shinto is primarily based on reverence for nature.

Shen-Tao

Until the sixth century AD the Japanese religion had no name. When Chinese Buddhism, Confucianism, and Taoism arrived, the Chinese called the Japanese religion, "Shen-Tao"—the way of the gods. Shinto is used to differentiate Japan's way from other religions.

Japan's openness allowed other beliefs to be assimilated into the Japanese way of life and thought. The

Japanese see no contradiction in combining religious forms. One can practice all religions without allegiance to any specific one.

Concepts and Beliefs

The moral and ethical life in Japan derives its strength from Confucian principles. Taoism's sense of harmony and balance influenced Japan's respect for nature. Buddhism assumed a unique form in Japan. The Buddhism which originated in China as Ch'an, came to be known in Japan as Zen. This is of particular interest because it is the form of Buddhism that has been introduced into Western spirituality.

Zen

Zen Buddhism advocates quietude through stillness and meditation, by becoming completely detached and utterly "thoughtless." This practice ultimately results in complete enlightenment. It is popular because it provides a calm atmosphere and discipline. Zen is practiced in monasteries under the direction of a mentor.

Beliefs in *kami* are evident all throughout the Japanese lifestyle. For the Japanese the environment and aesthetic surrounding is most important, as well as cleanliness and purity. Religion for the Japanese is not something to believe in, but a sense and "feel" for the spiritual dimension. The dead are presumed to remain close to the living and concerned for them. So ancestor worship has a prime place in Japan's religious sentiments. Homes have a special niche for the *kami* which are special to the family. Dead relatives and family members are remembered with a plaque. A Buddhist altar next to the Shinto shrine in the home invokes the *kami* as well as the Buddha.

Ancestor Worship

Shrines, Temples, Pilgrimages

Scattered throughout Japan, thousands of shrines dot the countryside. When people feel a need or have some special reason, they go to the shrine which is tended by Shinto priests. Although Shinto has no set rituals, when a person comes to a shrine for worship one follows specific customs and protocol. You enter the shrine through the sacred gateway, the *torii,* which separates the sacred from the mundane world. The *torii,* with its distinctive curved crossbars, identifies a shrine and is the universal symbol of Shinto.

Since cleanliness and purity are vital to the Japanese, one washes before prayer. One draws the attention of the *kami* by a clap of the hands. Since the *kami* has no physical representation, a mirror reflects the *kami's* goodness and light. A bell is rung and one silently prays. Often the worshiper will write the intention on a paper strip which graces the shrine. Shrine rituals usually are done by individuals. If one has a special intention, the shrine priest waves a wand over the worshiper as one prays to the *kami.* A Shinto priest ordinarily presides at shrines and acts as its caretaker.

Life Stages Celebrated

Shinto prescribes no obligatory rituals but individuals and families celebrate life events in a personal way by visiting a shrine. At birth and when one comes of age, the parents ask blessings from the Shinto priest. Special shrine celebrations mark one's third, fifth, and seventh birthdays.

As is the custom in the Orient, marriages are arranged by the parents. The ceremony, performed by a Shinto priest, is held in a special wedding hall, not at a shrine.

In Japan, everything is sacred. Japanese practices hint of religious overtones. For example, the Tea Ceremony, proper and elegant, emphasizes exactness, deliberation, and focus.

Japanese art is noted for its delicate and dainty brush strokes. Origami, the art of paper folding, is considered an art which fosters beauty and concentration. *Ikebana*, Japanese flower arranging, is replete with religious symbolism. Three flowers, strategically placed, are different heights. The tallest flower represents heaven. The second symbolizes humans, and the lowest flower honors the earth where the flower grew.

Spiritual Insights and Values

- Reverence for family and old age.
- Respect for nature and reverence for the environment.
- Politeness and deference to another.

PART THREE

Religions of the West

Ancient people solved life's mysteries with worship of many gods. While Abraham, a nomad in Ur between the Tigris and Euphrates rivers, wrestled with the questions of life through solitude and prayer, he encountered an overriding presence which revealed to him the one God. This experience was so compelling that Abraham obeyed the call to go to the land of Canaan. Abraham entered a covenant with this presence who eventually revealed his name to Moses as "Yahweh."

Abraham's relationship with the one God, continued throughout his life and the lives of succeeding generations. Abraham's faith experience and life, recorded in Genesis chapters 12—25, became the foundation of Judaism, Islam, and Christianity. Although each religion has its unique history, traditions, and practices, the three Semitic faiths acknowledge the one God known as "Yahweh" to Jews, "God" to Christians, and "Allah" to Muslims.

Judaism

We are familiar with Judaism because our Christian faith developed from Judaism and our practices adapt Jewish concepts. As the oldest of the monotheistic religions, Judaism derived from Abraham's experience of the one God. Judaism is not only a religion, but a way of life of a covenanted people invested with a specific mission from God. Their religion and their peoplehood are one and the same. The people fashioned the faith in God and the faith in God sustained the people.

History of Judaism

Descendants of Abraham

The Jewish story begins with Abraham, whose small family increased with the posterity of Isaac and Jacob. Israel's early history corresponds to the accounts of the chosen people and the kingdom of Israel found in the Bible until the Romans take over in 63 BC. Under the Romans, in AD 70, the Temple was destroyed and a new chapter in Jewish history began. The Jews were scattered in every direction, and the synagogue and prayer services replaced the Temple rituals.

Basic Beliefs

One God

The foundation of Judaism lies in the belief in one God who is the eternal, all-powerful, and loving Creator of all. This faith is expressed in the *Shema*, which begins, "Hear, O Israel, the LORD is our God, the Lord alone" (Deuteronomy 6:4). This concept of God introduced a revolutionary notion about God not residing in nature, but above nature as its creator.

Torah

The God of Israel engages in a personal relationship and covenant with Jews, revealing his nature through the

Scriptures and life events. God reaches out and shows humans how God's will is carried out in life. The Jews have a covenant responsibility to witness to God. Their identity and belonging controls daily life and worship.

Torah, "revealed teaching," in a strict sense refers to the first five books of the Bible. To be a faithful Jew, one's allegiance to Torah encompasses all life's activities. A Jew studies, prays, and lives Torah. The Torah scroll has remained for Jews a reliable assurance, taken along throughout their history as a portable homeland in the wanderings and the Diaspora. One's freedom and homeland can be confiscated, but what is in one's head and heart through ideas and the Torah cannot be seized.

Response to God

To be a Jew is to witness to God and the covenant. All Jewish life is governed by man's relationship with God. Jews do not ordinarily focus on the hereafter, but try to live responsibly in the world and respond to God by obeying the commandments in the Torah and Talmud (a record of the rabbis' discussion of the Torah). Jews believe that the world God created is good and to be enjoyed. The world is for us and we are to serve God by living according to God's law in the world.

Messiah

Messianism is central to Jewish faith as a hope that the prophets extolled. Some await the coming of a personal Messiah. Others see the establishment of the state of Israel as messianism fulfilled. Still others see messianism as God's kingdom on earth. For many Jews today, messianic expectations are spiritual and personal rather than an historic event.

Sacred Books   The Jews, along with Christians and Muslims, are called "People of the Book" because life is guided by the exhortations in the sacred writings. For Jews, the first five Books of the Bible—Genesis, Exodus, Leviticus, Numbers, and Deuteronomy—contain the crux of Jewish beliefs. The rest of the Hebrew Bible, called the *Tanakh,* consists of history, prophets, and writings. The Hebrew Bible is identical to the Christian Old Testament.

The Talmud, a multi-volume work, contains rabbinic interpretations, commentaries, and opinions to questions on how to carry out the 613 Torah commands. The Talmud undergoes constant scrutiny by rabbinic scholars about how best to carry out and apply the law to new situations.

Jewish Divisions According to Observance

Orthodox   Orthodox Judaism, the strictest form of Judaism, retains Hebrew in prayer and uses traditional forms of worship and practices. Orthodox Jews observe minute details of the Torah and Talmud and keep abreast by study in Jewish schools called Yeshivas. Orthodox rabbis are the only recognized religious authority in Israel.

Hasidic   Ultra-Orthodox Jews, the Hasidim, follow the law most meticulously. They live in close-knit communities and are recognized by distinctive garb. Men wear curled side locks, black suits, long coats, and large-brimmed hats. Women dress simply. In synagogue, men and women sit separately. The rabbi called "Rebbe" is more a spiritual mentor than a scholar. They are most noticeable in Jerusalem's *Mea Shearim* and in Manhattan. Those coming from eastern Europe speak Yiddish, a combination of German and Hebrew.

Conservative Jews, the majority of Jews in the United States today, strive to retain many traditions in modern living. They respect both the Torah and Talmud, but easily adapt to modern interpretations. They use both Hebrew and English in the synagogue and observe Jewish festivals.

Conservative

Reform Jews, progressive and liberal toward Jewish practices, reject what they consider outmoded laws and do not heed the Talmud. They consider the rabbi as a guide and call their places of worship Temples. Reform Jews adapt to modern-day practices, and their services may resemble Christian churches with hymns and organ music.

Reform

Secular Jews claim Jewish ancestry, but view Judaism as a culture, not a religion. They uphold the arts and culture, but do not follow the Torah or traditions.

Secular

Sanctification of Life

The birth of a child is especially joyful, because it means the Jewish heritage can continue. Boys are circumcised after eight days as a sign of God's covenant with Abraham. Girls are blessed and named at the Sabbath service. Jewish children receive a Hebrew name and a secular name.

Birth

To celebrate one's transition to adulthood, the *Bar Mitzvah* (son of the covenant) takes place when a boy reaches thirteen. After intense study of the Jewish religion, a boy reads from the Torah in the presence of the congregation and assumes his religious duties. A similar ceremony takes place when a girl reaches twelve, a *Bat Mitzvah* (daughter of the covenant), although among the Orthodox and Hasidic Jews, the girl is not permitted to

Coming of Age

take a role in a religious service. In Reform and Conservative synagogues, there is often a confirmation ceremony at about the age of sixteen or eighteen to affirm one's Jewishness. It usually takes place on Shavuot, the commemoration of the giving of the law on Sinai.

Marriage   Marriage is looked upon as a covenant between a man and a woman according to Genesis 1:28. It is the normal means for carrying on the Jewish heritage. A rabbi performs the marriage under a canopy, which symbolizes the new household. A glass crushed under foot reminds the newlyweds that life is fragile and sorrow comes amid joys. Intermarriage and divorce are discouraged.

Death,   Although many Jews believe in the immortality of the
Burial,   soul and the resurrection of the body, they emphasize
Kaddish   living one's life well and are not preoccupied with the hereafter. Ceremonies surrounding death show respect for the dead and console the living.

Burial takes place as soon as possible, to heed the biblical exhortation, "Return to dust." Jewish law discourages embalming or cremation. Immediate relatives tear their garments or wear an armband as a sign of mourning.

The *Kaddish*, a prayer recited at the funeral and on the anniversary of death, is an affirmation of life and asks God to take care of the deceased. After death the immediate family has a seven day period of morning called *Shiva*. They do not work and their mirrors are covered or reversed. They sit low on the floor and burn a memorial candle. Friends and relatives bring food for the mourners' consolation.

The *Yahrzeit*, death anniversary, is observed in synagogues where a plaque bears the names of deceased. Each time one visits the grave site, a stone is placed on the tombstone to show the deceased is not forgotten.

Prayer

Jews maintain a personal relationship with God through prayer both communal and personal. One's day is punctuated with prayer at specified times and anytime one wishes to reach out to God. Private prayer is the "heart's worship." Since all life is blessed, during the day a pious Jew acknowledges God's goodness and utters spontaneous praise with an oral affirmation a *B'rakah*—"Blessed are you, Lord, king of the Universe, who has blest me with (mention a specific blessing)."

Since humans are created by God with free will to choose between good and evil, a Jew consecrates good actions to God by *mitzvahs*. Each good deed and selfless action is a response to the covenant and strengthens one's Jewish commitment.

Synagogue

The synagogue is a place of prayer, study, and assembly. It is the house of God and humans. The diverse architectural designs reflect the locale. A rabbi, the head teacher of a synagogue, makes legal decisions and ordinarily officiates at weddings and funerals. A cantor is a professional who leads prayers and chanting during the service. Any lay person may read from the Torah.

In the synagogue the focal point is the Ark, a receptacle which houses the Torah scrolls. Used on Sabbath and festival days, the scrolls are encased in velvet surmounted with ornamental crowns to symbolize the royal dignity of the Scriptures.

A platform from which the Torah is read has a prominent place in the sanctuary. The *Ner Tamid*, an eternal light, is kept burning by the Ark out of respect for the word of God.

Rituals Although Jews can pray anywhere, communal prayer in the synagogue is held three times daily. For the prayer to take place a *minyan,* at least ten men, must be present. The official prayerbook called the *Siddur* contains the prayers used in the services. Once a year a burial takes place for worn Torahs, Bibles, and prayerbooks.

Festivals and Symbols

Celebrations Because Jews had no land or space to call their own for many years, time is a special gift of God and is sanctified with festival celebrations. Jews relive their history and strengthen their Jewish commitment in weekly Sabbath and holy day observances. Jewish observances bring together heaven and earth in celebration and remembrance. Jews look at the deeper meaning behind all their rituals. They do not celebrate events as past, but actively participate in events in the present.

Sabbath The Sabbath, the seventh day, is an oasis of prayer, study, and rest. It lasts from Friday sundown till Saturday sundown. It is not just a "do-nothing" day but one to honor God, evaluate one's life, and reflect on and affirm one's Jewish traditions. It is entirely "God's time" in which worldly cares are laid aside. Observant Jews refrain from work, travel, and business talk, among other things.

The Sabbath arrives as a welcome guest in the home in which the Sabbath atmosphere is sacred and holy. The mother of the household lights the Sabbath candles and shields her eyes to separate the worldly week from the sacred. A festive meal, prepared beforehand, is eaten in an atmosphere of worship, relaxation, and Sabbath songs. The father honors his wife by reading Proverbs, chapter 31. He blesses the Sabbath bread, wine, and the children. Sabbath services in the synagogue take place on Friday evening and Saturday morning. The Sabbath concludes with prayers and blessing of wine and fragrant spices, so that the aroma of the Sabbath may continue throughout the week. So that the Sabbath continues into the week, one tries to catch the Sabbath candle reflection in one's fingernail.

Rosh Hashanah, the Jewish new year, presents an opportunity to look back and to resolve to do better in the year ahead. A call to repentance on the *shofar*, a ram's horn, is blown in memory of the ram used as a substitute sacrifice instead of Abraham's son.

Rosh
Hashanah

On Rosh Hashanah, Jews celebrate creation and give thanks for life's good things by eating a mixture of apples and honey. Observant Jews toss bread crumbs into a stream so one's sins be washed away during the ten "Days of Awe," between New Year and Yom Kippur, when Jews reexamine their lives and recommit themselves to the covenant.

Yom Kippur, the Day of Atonement, is a strict fast day, on which Jews atone not only for personal sins but for the sins of humanity. They use the day as a time of annual spiritual renewal and visit the grave site of loved ones. The *Kol Nidre,* a somber haunting melody, begs God for release from all debts and vows. The Book of Jonah is read to remind all that God is good to the repentant. The blowing of the *shofar* at the day's end signifies closing of the Book of Judgment.

Yom Kippur

Other Festivals   Rosh Hashanah and Yom Kippur are purely religious holidays. The Jews also celebrate: Sukkoth, Simhat Torah, Shavout, Hanukkah, and Purim.

Symbols of the Covenant and Jewish Identity

Star of David   The Star of David, the noblest Jewish symbol, graces the Israeli flag and reminds Jews of their covenant with God. Two equilateral triangles intertwined form six points. The one triangle represents the basic units of the universe—God, the world, and humans. The second triangle represents that which binds them together—creation, revelation, and redemption. God made the world in creation, chooses humans through revelation to be co-workers in the act of redemption in the world.

Tablets and Menorah   Tablets with the commandments inscribed with Hebrew numerals remind Jews of the Commandments given at Sinai. This symbol is commonly used in synagogue decor or pendants. The Menorah is a multi-branched candelabra used at Hanukkah. It reminds Jews that amid the darkness of life's darkest moments, there always is hope in the bright light of God's redeeming love.

Kippah   Observant Jewish men, who believe man is under God's protection and a man's head needs be covered at all times, usually wear a small skull cap. Others wear it only for prayer. This shows that man is always subject to God and wearing of the skull cap in public is an easy identification of Jewishness.

Spiritual Insights and Values
- Pride in one's heritage.
- Generosity and philanthropy.
- Love of learning.

Christianity

Christianity, the largest and most widespread world religion, began with the life and mission of Jesus. Christians believe Jesus to be the promised Messiah and the Son of God. "God so loved the world that he gave his only Son..." (John 3:16).

Origins of Christianity

Christianity did not develop in a vacuum, but originated within the Jewish faith community. Christianity provided a revolutionary approach to the sacred and established a new covenant with God through the person and teachings of Jesus. He began his mission of teaching and healing when John the Baptist baptized him in the Jordan River as a sign of his humanity, "[T]hough he was in the form of God, he did not deem equality with God as something to be exploited, but emptied himself..." (Philippians 2:6). Jesus came into this world as a Jew and lived a poor modest life in Nazareth of Galilee as an observant Jew.

Jesus of Nazareth

At first, Christianity was preached to the Jews, but then the Christian faith spread to the lands around the Mediterranean through the missionary efforts of Saint Paul. Greek, Roman, and Egyptian mystery religions existed and dominated the cultural landscape. Thought patterns and ideas became readily adopted and assimilated by the Christians in their worship and rituals.

Worldwide Message

A Christian's faith is based on the life, mission, and teachings of Jesus and revolves around the Good News Jesus brought—that the Father loves us and our sins can be forgiven. Through the passion, death, and resurrection of Jesus, our sins are forgiven and we can be united with Jesus in heaven.

Constantine

The early Christians, though in the minority, proved zealous in the faith, especially their steadfast courage during the persecutions (200-312). Constantine (d. 337), in 312, proclaimed religious freedom in the Edict of Milan.

Christianity, although plagued internally with theological differences and heresies, remained united as the faith Christ proclaimed. In 381, Emperor Theodosius authorized Christianity as the official religion of the Roman Empire.

Early Schism

For the first thousand years, Christianity was united, although the faith was expressed in two divergent ways—the East and the West. Theological tensions between the Christian East and the West escalated and in 1054 a split occurred. The Christians in the East became known as the Orthodox Church with Constantinople, formerly Byzantium, as the center. The Christians in the West became known as the Roman Catholic Church. The city of Rome became, and today remains, the hub of the Roman Catholic Church.

Later Schism

Another rupture in Christianity occurred in 1517. The Protestant Reformation spawned the many Protestant denominations.

Common Elements of Christian Belief

Jesus
Scripture
Community

Generally Christians agree on some basic doctrine such as the divinity of Jesus, the division of sacred Scriptures into the Old and New Testaments, and the preaching of Jesus as a model for life. All Christians worship God, in a community of faith, on the Lord's Day.

Christians strive to live the moral life Jesus taught, especially through love of God and neighbor. All accept Jesus' teaching on forgiveness and compassion. All believe they are called to spread the Good News of Jesus. Christians believe that, like Christ, one must be concerned about the welfare of others and so hospitals, schools, and relief organizations are under Christian auspices.

Love of God and Neighbor

The Christian calendar commemorates the life of Christ throughout the year. Advent is a four-week period of preparation for Christmas on December 25. Epiphany, celebrated twelve days later, recalls the visit of the wise men to the infant Jesus. Lent, a forty-day period of penance, begins on Ash Wednesday and prepares Christians for the major holy day, Easter Sunday, which celebrates Christ's Resurrection. Pentecost, fifty days after Easter Sunday, commemorates the coming of the Holy Spirit upon the apostles. Most Christians celebrate these feasts in various ways. Scattered throughout the year are the commemorations of the saints.

Christian Feasts

The challenge of Christianity for all who claim allegiance to Christian standards, lies in one's faith and intention to strive to bring goodness into the world. Many Christians are Christian because the faith was passed on as their religious heritage from their parents. To be Christian of the more than 300 denominations is to live according to the life and example of Jesus. If we examine the Christian denominations closer, we discover that we have much more in common than we realize.

Challenge of Christianity

The Major Divisions of Christianity

The Roman Catholic Church

The Roman Catholic Church traces its origins back to Jesus himself who gave Peter the authority to continue his mission. The pope, the bishop of Rome, is the successor to Peter and the bishops succeed the apostles in preserving the traditions and teachings of the Church.

Roman Catholics believe their faith has retained an unbroken line of authority from the apostles to the present. Catholics believe the way to know God is through the life and teachings of Jesus as presented in Scripture and Tradition, as well as the teaching authority of the Catholic Church.

Catholics and other Christians believe we know God through the words and deeds of Jesus. Jesus' life and mission stands out as the example to follow to come close to God. In affirming that Jesus shows forth the power of God, he is the Savior who came to earth and gave his life for the salvation of all peoples. Jesus is the "way, the truth, and the life" (John 14:6).

The main focus of Roman Catholic worship is the Mass, which is the reenactment of Jesus' sacrifice on the cross. Through words of consecration of ordained priests, Catholics believe the bread and wine are transformed into the Body and Blood of Christ. The real Presence of Jesus continues in the consecrated hosts which Catholics receive in holy Communion and preserve in tabernacles in Catholic churches.

Catholics believe they participate in Jesus' life and grace through seven sacraments: baptism, confirmation, holy Eucharist, reconciliation, sacrament of the sick, holy orders, and matrimony.

Roman Catholics regard Mary, the Mother of God and

Jesus, with special esteem and honor her in many feasts. Catholics also believe in the virgin birth—that is, Jesus was born of the Virgin Mary.

Roman Catholics honor those persons who most faithfully lived up to Christian ideals. The Church canonizes them and they receive the title "saint." Throughout the liturgical year, Catholics honor them in the liturgy and in private prayer. Catholics believe that saints in heaven can assist us on earth by their intercession.

Since the Catholic Church was "updated" in Vatican II, there have been many changes in thought and practice. The Catholic Church continues to be the largest branch of Christianity.

The Eastern Orthodox Church also traces its origins to apostolic times when the gospel and message of Jesus reached Asia Minor, Greece, and eastern Europe.

Orthodox Church

From the earliest days of Christianity, the message of Jesus fit into the local culture. Language, rituals, and theology developed in various ways because of differences in culture. In the fourth century, the Roman empire split into East and West. The East comprised Greek-speaking nations: Greece, Egypt, Asia minor, and eastern Europe. The Latin West included Italy, Gaul, Spain, and parts of Great Britain.

The Church in the East, centered in Constantinople, preserved loyalty to both the Emperor and Rome. The East developed independently from the West, but regarded the Patriarch of Constantinople an equal with the Bishop of Rome as head of the Church. For the first thousand years, Christianity was united in basic doctrine, although differences in language, ritual, and culture existed between the East and the West.

Gradually differences in doctrinal interpretation

heightened tensions between East and West. Tensions escalated when Constantine, in the fourth century, moved his capital to Byzantium (now Istanbul, Turkey). In 1054 the patriarch of the East and the bishop of Rome both claiming supremacy, mutually excommunicated each other. The definitive split occurred in 1204 when the Crusaders ransacked Constantinople.

Orthodox theology and liturgy stresses the mystical awesome presence of God with incense, chanting, and processions. The melodic polyphonic *a capella* choir harmony is a memorable experience and the pride of the smallest parish. Orthodox priests can marry, but bishops are chosen from celibate monks.

The Orthodox Church is nearest to Roman Catholics in doctrine and practices. Recognition of the pope as the supreme head is the chief obstacle to the orthodox being one with Rome.

Protestantism Although Protestantism is the overall term for churches formed as a result of the Reformation in 1517, other churches fall under the aegis "Protestant." For several hundred years, reformers decried abuses of the Catholic Church. Generally, the Protestant churches developed in four different movements: Lutheran, Calvinist, Anglican, and Anabaptist.

Martin Luther, a Catholic priest, wishing to rectify abuses in the church, pinned 95 theses on the cathedral door in Wittenberg. He did not intend to begin a church but to debate and draw attention to the abuses and so reform the Catholic Church. His action precipitated other reactions which spread all over Europe.

Presbyterians grew out of the Reformation efforts of Calvin, Zwingli and Knox. They believed in shared power of governing in the church.

King Henry VIII when denied a divorce in 1534, set himself up as the head of the Church of England. Anglicans preserved the liturgy of the Catholic Church, but refused to accept the supremacy of the pope. When the followers came to America they became known as Episcopalians. Methodists, Quakers, and the Salvation Army developed from the Anglican split.

Anabaptists believe that baptism should be administered only to adults. They also uphold strict separation of church and state and pacifism. Amish and Mennonites uphold Anabaptist teachings.

Soon Protestant churches mushroomed throughout Europe and spread into America. When churches disagreed on points of doctrine or leadership, they split and began another Protestant church. That's why there are hundreds of Protestant denominations.

Other churches, independently founded in America, claim Christian ideals, but are not results of the Reformation. The Mormons, Church of Jesus Christ of Latterday Saints, developed from Joseph Smith's experiences, in 1827, of receiving the Book of Mormon from the angel Moroni.

Adventist millenialism stressed belief in the immanent end of the world and second coming of Christ. In 1855, Mary Ellen White began the Seventh Day Adventists when she had a revelation that the second coming of Christ would occur only when the seventh day would be the Christian holy day, and not Sunday.

Jehovah's Witnesses, a millennial church, began in 1874, when Charles Russell made several predictions of the end of the world. Jehovah's Witnesses emphasize the Old Testament, refuse to participate in military service, and deny the Trinity. Their places of worship are called Kingdom Halls.

Christian Scientists believe in healing through prayer because of Mary Baker Eddy's cure in 1879. She wrote *Science and Health with Key to the Scriptures* to advocate healing through spiritual means and reading. This religion is propagated through Christian Science reading rooms in public areas.

Spiritual Insights and Values

- Respect and awe at the liturgy.
- Love of rituals and processions.
- Devotion and reverence of icons.
- Love and knowledge of sacred Scripture.
- Generosity in tithing and contributing.
- Spirit of evangelization and hospitality.

Islam

With over a billion adherents Islam is the youngest monotheistic religion which looks to Abraham as the "father in faith" and which believes in the same God as the Jews and Christians. As the fastest growing religion, Islam, second in size to Christianity, is global, practiced in almost every country, and dominant in about fifty countries. Islam includes a wide range of national, ethnic, social, and linguistic backgrounds from North Africa, the Near East, Indonesia, Malaysia, and the Philippines. Muslims today also have a presence in Europe and North America.

Origins of Islam

Islam stems from the root word "salam" and literally means, "Peaceful surrender and submission to Allah." One who follows Islam is a Muslim, "one who submits." We begin our journey into Islam late in the sixth century AD in the desert region of Saudi Arabia, Mecca, which served as a crossroads for caravan trade routes to the East linking Syria, Palestine, Egypt, and Iraq with lands in the Far East. Mecca thrived not only as a busy commercial center, but served as a polytheistic haven where many idols were housed and venerated in numerous shrines, especially in a large cubical edifice, the *Ka'aba,* which Muslims believe was built by Abraham. Mecca also had an active political structure which hosted seasonal tribal assemblies. It is from this varied background that Islam developed and drew its ethical principles and enduring vigor.

Mecca

The story of Islam begins with a young Arab, Muhammad (d. AD 632), who was orphaned at a tender age and raised by relatives. Known for his uprightness and honesty, he was hired by and subsequently married a wealthy caravan owner, Khadija, fifteen years his senior.

Muhammad

Contemplative by nature, Muhammad often sought spiritual solitude in a nearby cave. When Muhammad was forty, in AD 610, he experienced mystical visions and voices. For over twenty years these spiritual encounters through the angel Gabriel revealed and dictated the words of the one God, Allah. At first, Muhammad thought he was going mad, but persistent revelations and affirmation by his family assured him that Allah really called him. Although Muhammad was illiterate, he recited the revelations to companions who recorded them on leaves, stones, or bones. Later these were compiled in the Qur'an, the sacred book of Islam.

Muhammad was not well-received in Mecca because he berated the people for their worship of idols and thus threatened their economic security. Knowing of Muhammad's upright reputation, the people of Medina invited him to their city, about two hundred miles north of Mecca. This flight in AD 622, the *Hegira,* marks the beginning of Islam and the Islamic new year. In AD 630, Muhammad marched back into Mecca, converted the Meccans, and purged the *Ka'aba* of all idols. He died in AD 632, in Medina after he delivered a touching farewell at Arafat, which today is commemorated during the pilgrimage.

At Muhammad's death, Islam had spread across the Arabian peninsula. Within a hundred years Islam extended from Arabia into northern Africa and Spain. The rapid spread of Islam is due to the militant directness and simplicity of its message. Muslims consider it an act of faith and divine mandate to spread their religion and convert peoples. Islam provided a stability and surety to nomadic peoples, torn between many ideologies. This tribal mentality explains Muslim cohesiveness.

Sacred Presence of Allah

Qur'an   The Qur'an is the main source revealing how Allah expects Muslims to live. The Qur'an is so respected that Allah's words are considered a sacred and divine presence. It is the symbol and embodiment of the intimate relationship between God and humans. The Qur'an literally means recitation. Muslims believe it is the absolute word of God actually spoken to Muhammad who served as the vehicle through which God's word was transmitted. Because Muhammad came into contact with Jews and Christians while he was a camel driver, the Qur'an contains stories included in the Hebrew and Christian Scriptures, although details both differ.

Since the original language was Arabic, Muslims consider the Arabic Qur'an to be the only authentic version. Translations are not considered inspired. Muslims believe one gains spiritual merit from the Qur'an, whether it is sung, recited, memorized, chanted, or prayed.

Muslims believe in the physical sacredness of the book of the Qur'an. One handles the Qur'an only after one washes and purifies oneself. Anyone who does not respect the Qur'an as the word of God is not to handle the book.

Hadith

Muhammad's sayings, advice, way of life, and traditions are in the *Hadith*. It comprehensively covers all aspects of life and aids Muslims to realize how Muhammad thought, spoke, and conducted his affairs. Along with the Qur'an, the *Hadith* provides spiritual and practical guidance on how to live as a faithful Muslim.

Shari'ah

The Law of Islam, *Shari'ah,* spells out in detail and deals with all matters which reflect the Islamic way of life. It deals with issues and questions that arise as to how to act and behave. The interpretations of law vary greatly because schools of interpretation take on the character of the nation and a particular age.

There is no separation of religion and state—religion, politics, and society are all interconnected. Because Islam spread through many countries and cultures, Islamic scholars interpreted the code of laws accordingly.

Basic Beliefs in Islam

Allah
Islamic faith centers on the One Supreme Being, Allah, as the merciful and compassionate creator and judge of all human actions. Islam derives its way of life and practices from exhortations and directives set forth in the revelations to Muhammad recorded in the Qur'an. Muslims do not believe in intermediary intercessors, because Allah alone can forgive sin.

Muslims honor Allah alone and so there are no representations in icons or images of humans or animals. Muslim decor involves geometric patterns and calligraphic designs, especially with scripts from the Qur'an.

Islam believes that all are to be converted to Allah. There is special consideration for Jews and Christians who already know the one God (Allah) in their traditions. Obedience to Allah is the key concept and extends into the political and secular sphere of a Muslim's life.

Angels
Angels were created from light and serve as messengers to humans. Four angels are named. First, there is Michael who defeats Satan. The second, Gabriel, God's messenger, appeared to Muhammad and dictated the Qur'an. He also announced the birth of Jesus to the Virgin Mary. The third angel named is Uriel who will sound the trumpet on the last day. Finally, there is Azrael who is the angel of death. Every human being also has two guardian angels.

Human Life
Human life, the creation of Allah, is a transitory gift of the creator to humans. The Qur'an places a high priority on life and its preservation. Procreation is considered an important aspect of marriage. Abortion in Islam is considered homicide, except therapeutic abortion.

Muslims believe that the prophets reveal God's presence among the people and believe each prophet came
for a specific mission to a specific people. The Qu'ran
names twenty-five messengers and prophets from God
as authorized spokespersons for God. Most of these include biblical persons such as Adam, Noah, Abraham,
Moses, Job, Jonah, Ishmael, David, Solomon, John the
Baptist, and Jesus. Muhammad is the last and seal of the
prophets. Islam holds that Allah revealed himself to the
Jewish prophets and to Jesus. Jews and Christians are
considered the "People of the Book."

Once one submits to Allah, whatever happens is for
the best. This is not fatalism or predestination, but all is
foreordained by the will of Allah. Man is held account-
able for all his actions in this life by the judgment. Jesus
will usher in the last days when Allah will judge men's
deeds. The good will be rewarded with heaven and the
evil will be punished in hell.

Islam's Pillars of Faith

"There is no god but Allah and Muhammad is his
prophet" is the chief act of faith and encompasses the
essence of Islamic belief. Recited in every prayer and
many times daily by a devout Muslim, this profession of
faith is the single sentence one recites in the presence of
two adult believers to become a Muslim. One who recites the profession of faith with conviction and sincer-
ity becomes a Muslim in the eyes of divine law.

It affirms the two basic Islamic beliefs. God is one,
absolute, supreme, creator, and judge. Muhammad is
Allah's mouthpiece. God's love and compassionate mercy
is the foremost divine quality they respect. The *shahadah,*
the first phrase spoken by angel Gabriel to Muhammad,

is said into the ears of a newborn and recited when one is dying.

Daily Prayer (Salah)

Prayer is the chief ritual and act of worship for Muslims. In Muslim countries a muezzin announces the call to prayer from the minaret, the tower of the mosque. The prayer lasts about ten minutes and can be recited alone or with others. Before their prayer, Muslims take off their shoes and purify themselves with either water or sand. At mosque entrances, a fountain or pool is handy to wash one's face, hands, arms, and feet. They purify the outside body as well as inside their soul. They shed their shoes much like Moses at the burning bush, for it is "holy ground." For this purpose they use a prayer rug to sanctify the place of prayer. Most Muslims carry a stone from a sacred Muslim site on which they place their head as they prostrate, to show humility.

Muslims pray a specific prayer with its attending gestures five times a day at sunrise, noon, middle of the afternoon, sunset, and on retiring. The ritual is exact and regulated. One faces Mecca and puts hands to one's ears, then to one's face with a series of bows and full prostrations. Islamic prayers primarily are prayers of thanks and praise of Allah, not of intercession.

Almsgiving (Zakah)

Muslims share a portion of their worldly goods with the less fortunate as stipulated by their faith. In some countries, the *Zakah* is a fixed tax but voluntary giving is always encouraged. The alms shared is not that which costs the most but that which is given with the greatest fervor. Alms given freely merit one atonement for sin. Spontaneous alms are especially meritorious only if given discreetly, without fanfare.

During Ramadan, the ninth month of the Muslim calendar when the Qur'an revelations began, those able are required to abstain completely from food, drink, smoking, and sex from sunrise to sunset. This fasting requires self-mastery and discipline, but is a time of grace and religious fervor. Since Muslims follow a lunar year, Ramadan occurs at different seasons. It challenges one's stamina, especially when Ramadan falls during oppressively hot summers. Each evening brings respite when a Muslim may eat.

On the last day of Ramadan, the feast of breaking the fast, *Id al-Fit'r,* begins with a special morning prayer in the mosque followed by three days of feasting, celebrating, visiting friends, gift-giving, and sharing.

Muslims look forward to the pilgrimage as a once-in-a lifetime event. If one is financially and physically able, a Muslim is obliged to make a pilgrimage to Mecca at least once in their lifetime during the month of pilgrimage. Devout Muslims believe if they die on the *Hajj*, they gain greater eternal rewards. This trek, which brings millions of Muslims from all over the world to Mecca, demonstrates Muslim solidarity and unity. Anyone not a Muslim is barred from entering Mecca, the most sacred Islamic city. Although the journey today is not as arduous because of rapid air travel, the rites and ceremonies of the twelve-day *Hajj* require much stamina and physical strength, since pilgrims observe a strict fast as during Ramadan.

Fasting
(Sawm)

Pilgrimage
(Hajj)

Other Common Elements of Islam

Mosque and Friday Prayer

On Fridays, a devout Muslim joins in community prayer in the mosque at which an Imam, a learned scholar, usually delivers a sermon. The men kneel in neat rows with women in the back, as they face the *mihrab* or niche which points in the direction of Mecca.

Friday is the Muslims weekly holy day, but not a day of rest. Muslims do not consider it a "work-free" day because God never ceases to work. Muslims have no common ritual except the Friday noon prayer which Muslims consider as a communal direct contact with Allah.

Jihad

Although considered by many to be the sixth pillar of faith, the concept of *jihad* has never been a clear-cut issue. Over the years jihad includes a wide range of meanings and interpretations. To refer to jihad only as a holy war is misleading. In its original meaning, which Muhammad defined, jihad is the struggle against evil both in one's own soul and in society. Muslims believe their religion brings peace through struggles against evil.

Women, Festivals, Symbols

Muhammad raised the status of women in Islamic society. Previously, baby girls were murdered or left to die. Women are respected as those whose duty is in the home. They are not encouraged to pray in the mosques, although they may.

Islam's identifying symbol consists of a crescent new moon encircling a single star. The new moon and stars are crucial for nomadic peoples who looked to the heavens for directions, and as signals to guide them in observing their festivals. This identifying Islamic symbol graces the domes of mosques and on flags of Islamic countries. Another sacred symbol is the calligraphic form of the *shahadah,* the Islamic profession of faith.

Division of Islam

Sunnis depend on the consensus of the community and norms based on the traditions of Muhammad for guidance. Their religious leaders do not need to be descendants of Muhammad. Sunni is the main division of Islam. About 80 percent of Muslims belong to the Sunnis, the "people of the tradition."

Sunni

Shi'ites are the minority. About 20 percent of Muslims are Shi'ite. They reside mostly in Iran and southern Iraq. They originally looked to religious leaders in the family of Muhammad to provide leadership for them. They consider Ali, a cousin of Muhammed, as the first Caliph or leader of all Muslims. When the line of Ali became extinct, a council choose a supreme Imam, often called Ayatollah, as leader. They continue that practice today.

Shi'ite

Spiritual Insights and Values

- Devotion to prayer.
- Personal surrender to God.
- Respect for ritual and correctness.

PART FOUR

The Catholic Church and Other Religions

A s we conclude our odyssey, a broad historical perspective can help us understand how the Catholic Church has evolved in its attitude toward other religions.

Early History of Ecumenism

The Church reacted to the Protestant Reformation with a counterreformation, the Council of Trent (1545-1563), which issued authoritative defenses against heresy. The Church held to a rigid orthodoxy against the reformers, while at the same time addressing some of the abuses that caused the Reformation. The council addressed the abuses by regulating all Church laws, rituals, and practices, while at the same time rejecting the doctrine of the reformers. The Church considered other religions false and Catholics did not associate with outsiders.

Intolerance continued, and the Catholic Church harbored a closed attitude toward other religions well into the twentieth century. Cautious and wary of any changes, the Church found it difficult to adopt new ways of thinking. The Church was catapulted into the modern age with technology, science, and communications systems rapidly shrinking the world. A radical change was imminent!

Ecumenism in Vatican II

In 1959, Pope John XXIII called an ecumenical council, Vatican II. This council opened the doors and windows of the Church. The task was to relate to and understand the problems confronting the Church.

Documents of Vatican II

The sixteen documents of Vatican II provide new insights and approaches to the Church's identity and mission. There was a new effort to relate to other religions and understand them. Breakthroughs in ecumenical understanding led to greater tolerance and openness. The documents of the council demonstrate the growing understanding of believer and nonbeliever alike.

Dogmatic Constitution on the Church (*Lumen Gentium*)

The Savior wills everyone to be saved....Nor is God remote from those who in shadows and images seek the unknown God....There are those who, through no fault of their own, do not know the gospel of Christ or his church but who nevertheless seek God with a sincere heart, and moved by grace, try in their actions to do his will as they know it through the dictates of their conscience—these too may attain eternal salvation.

Article 16

The one mediator, Christ, established and constantly sustains here on earth his holy church....This is the unique church of Christ which in the Creed we profess to be one, holy, catholic and apostolic....This church, constituted and organized as a society in the present world, subsists in the Catholic Church....Nevertheless, many elements of sanctification and truth are found outside its visible confines. Since these are gifts belonging to the church of Christ, they are forces impelling towards catholic unity.

Article 8

Throughout history, to the present day, there is found among different peoples a certain awareness of a hidden power, which lies behind the course of nature and the events of human life....This awareness and recognition results in a way of life that is imbued with a deep religious sense....The Catholic Church rejects nothing of what is true and holy in these religions. It has high regard for the manner of life and conduct, the precepts and doctrines which, although differing in many ways from its own teaching, nevertheless often reflect a ray of that truth which enlightens all men and women.

Article 2

Declaration on the Relation of the Church to Non-Christian Religions (*Nostra Aetate*)

The Vatican council declares that the human person has a right to religious freedom. Freedom of this kind means that everyone should be immune from coercion by individuals, social groups, and every human power so that, within due limits, no men or women are forced to act against their convictions nor are any persons to be restrained from

Declaration on Religious Liberty (*Dignitatis Humanae*)

acting in accordance with their convictions in religious matters....

Article 2

Paul VI and John Paul II

Pope Paul VI who became pope in 1963 continued the work of Vatican II. In his encyclical, *Ecclesiam Suam,* he encouraged the ecumenical spirit, "The Church must enter into dialogue with the world in which it lives. It has something to say, a message to give a communication to make" (n. 65).

In his lengthy reign, Pope John Paul II has expanded the Church's outreach in numerous creative ways. Not only in his writings and encyclicals but in more than a hundred trips to all corners of the globe.

At the mosque in Damascus, Syria, the pope asked forgiveness for atrocities committed against Muslims. On a visit to Indonesia, which is 90 percent Muslim, the pope noted, "Let us serve the God we have come to know in a spirit of dialogue, respect, and cooperation."

On his visit to Cameroon, John Paul II was persuaded better interfaith relations are necessary when a local dignitary observed, "We know we're divided, but we don't know why" (see *Crossing The Threshold of Hope*, 148).

Ecumenism and the Church Today

At times we can have the impression that Catholics are opposed to mixing with other religions because Jesus said, "I am the way and the truth and the life" (John 14:6a). Jesus challenges his followers to a radical commitment. Jesus intended to found a Church that would continue to proclaim the truth to the whole world.

The Catholic Church Is Missionary

The Catholic Church is by nature missionary and it takes the mandate of Jesus most seriously: "Go therefore and made disciples of all nations, baptizing them in the name of the Father and of the Son and of the Holy Spirit" (Matthew 28:19).

Does this directive from Jesus disallow Catholics to mingle with other faiths? Absolutely not! This mandate challenges Catholics to be so committed that they attract others to the faith just by their behavior, as the early Christians attracted others to the faith.

Being missionary does not mean roping everyone in to my way of worship or thinking. Nor does it uproot one from a sincere religious commitment of another faith and transplant it into my way. It is God who calls us into the Church. Being a missionary means to share the good news which is, love the Lord your God with all your heart and love your neighbor as yourself (see Matthew 22:37-39). This is the core of the Christian message. Our task is to grace the world with our best selves, making our niche of the world a fertile place for the love of God to grow.

Evangelization

To evangelize means to live in such a wholesome way that others are drawn to and encouraged in their faith. Others are attracted to faith by example, not by direct tactics. True evangelization draws the godliness out of people, and does not pour religion and our way into them.

The effort of evangelization aims first to bring back into the faith lapsed and inactive Catholics and to welcome those who have no religious affiliation or commitment. The American bishops' pastoral *To the Ends of the*

Earth stresses, "Mission is not the power and need to dominate,…but a profound respect for the ways others have already searched for and experienced God" (n. 32).

Fostering an Interreligious Understanding

A touching anecdote can help us better understand the impact of interreligious understanding. A Protestant minister, a Jewish rabbi, and a Catholic priest served as chaplains in the same unit during World War II. Their friendship was so strong that they pledged that if one of them should die in battle, the other two would provide an honorable funeral.

The Jewish rabbi was killed and, true to their word, the two survivors sought a Jewish cemetery. There was none, so they requested a burial site from the local pastor for their friend. "I must first check the books to see if a Jew can be buried in a Catholic cemetery." After consulting the rules, the priest informed them, "He can't be buried in the blessed ground, but he can be laid to rest outside the gate." That's where he was buried.

Years later the priest and minister decided to visit the grave of their dear friend, but they could not find it. They asked the aging pastor what happened to the grave outside the gate. He replied, "I used to look at that grave sadly for it seemed so cold and alone. I again looked in the books. In no place did it say the fence couldn't be moved. And that's what I did—I moved the fence."

We often need to move fences to foster greater understanding. We must remove the fence of prejudice. Prejudice stems from ignorance. The more we know about another, the more tolerant we will be.

We should tear down the fence of ignorance by learning about other religions, why they do what they do. We can learn about what they believe and how they express their faith. We must move the fence of self-righteousness. We should not belittle the faith others have, even though we disagree or find their practices strange. Catholic customs also may appear strange to those who do not understand.

Stereotypes and false generalizations divide us from one another. How easily we form stereotyped ideas regarding religion, especially from hearsay or the media. It is important for us to realize that within a religion there is a whole gamut of differences and degrees. Not all persons practice religion with the same fervor.

Building Bridges of Dialogue and Understanding

Recall the popular song, "Getting to Know You," by Oscar Hammerstein. Make the first gesture to become acquainted with other faiths. Initiate ways to approach and befriend others.

Cultivate friendships with persons of other faiths and do not be intimidated to speak of and witness to your own beliefs. Learn about the other's faith experience.

Realize that one opens up to the God one has come to know. When Lillian Carter was a Peace Corps volunteer in India, she noted, "The Hindu prays to his god; and mine answers." Other faiths need not be a threat to our faith, but a challenge and opportunity for us to be enriched.

Religious differences are not as disastrous as are religious indifference and apathy. Cultivate an active interest and approachability about religious issues. Brush up on main points of your faith. Be prepared to answer questions prefaced with, "Why do Catholics…?" Being conversant about your own faith will enable you to share it more accurately in a way that interests others.

Realize that most religious differences are based on

one's outlook rather than on animosity. Recognize the unity and commonality that already exists between religions. Most religions agree in more points than those in which they disagree.

Take advantage of opportunities to share your faith as well as share what you know about the other's faith. Heed the scriptural admonition, "Always be ready to make your defense to anyone who demands from you an accounting for the hope that is in you; yet do it with gentleness and reverence" (1 Peter 3:15-16a).

Search out ways to be enriched and to enrich others. Although an ordinary Catholic feels incompetent to engage in deep theological discussion, one ought to make it a point to learn and be conversant in one's own faith. Chance encounters provide occasions for spontaneous interfaith understanding: while riding a bus, waiting in line at the supermarket, and greeting a person on the street. Casual encounters prove more beneficial than planned agendas.

Learn about the customs and traditions of others and ask questions which give the impression you want to learn and not threaten. Attend a service of another denomination and discover how others pray and worship. Remember, a Catholic does not receive communion in a Protestant church. Organize a faith-sharing group of diverse religions.

Some Final Thoughts

Let us follow the wise advice of Mahatma Gandhi, the great advocate of nonviolence, "I open my windows and doors and allow all cultures and religions to blow about freely; but I refuse to be swept off my feet by any."

It is not necessary that we all sing the same song, but the music we make to honor our God ought to blend into a harmony of peace, understanding, and love. Avery Cardinal Dulles, SJ, in an ecumenical address asserted, "To be truly catholic, in the literal sense of the word, means to be open to all truth and goodness from whatever source it comes."

Our faith will be enriched and expanded when we can see God through others' faith lenses. Our personal faith must be open enough, vulnerable enough, and sincere enough to allow another's belief to speak to us without fear or hesitancy.

If we have an open ecumenical spirit, we will be able to swim in the faith pool of the other. When buoyed up with the life jacket of our faith and values, we can go with the tide and float freely with no fear of being submerged and be refreshed in our own faith. Our human future depends on our ability to live at peace with our own center as well as with the centers other than our own.

The Dalai Lama has some closing observations: "Every religion of the world has similar ideals of love, the same goal of benefitting humanity through spiritual practice, and the same effect of making their followers into better human beings."

Prayer for a True Interreligious Understanding

Lord, help me to appreciate the hunger for the divine which is deep within each heart; help me understand that in the many and often strange ways peoples have expressed their faith, the believer is sincere, and deserves my love, respect, and understanding.

Help me realize that each soul who acts in the name of religion is sincere and wishes to communicate with the divine in whatever form one perceives. Give to me the openness and wonder of children for whom any manifestation of the divine is a miracle. Let me heed the spirit of the poet W. B. Yeats: "Step lightly; you tread on noble dreams." Let me build bridges of tolerance, acceptance, and respect in my dealings with others.

Loving God, we believe you live among us and care for us. We believe that where you are is holy ground. We realize you love all people and that their ways and lands are also holy.

Help us discover your wonders and mystery in the lives and stories of other people as they struggle to do good as they perceive it. Help us realize that other people do differ with us with a contrasting world view and attitude and notion of how God is to be worshiped.

Send your enlightening spirit to guide us so we may listen, learn, understand, and be open to your presence in all human endeavors called "religion." Let us realize that all other religions are sacred and holy ground and we pray that we may step reverently into the sacred world of other religions. Amen.

Other Titles of Interest...

What You Should Know About Church History
Charlene Altemose, MSC
#67955 • $4.95

What You Should Know About the Mass
Charlene Altemose, MSC
#68010 • $3.95

What You Should Know About the Sacraments
Charlene Altemose, MSC
#68035 • $4.95

What You Should Know About Mary
Charlene Altemose, MSC
#68005 • $5.95

What You Should Know About the Saints
Charlene Altemose, MSC
#68050 • $5.95

What You Should Know About Angels
Charlene Altemose, MSC
#67950 • $4.95

What You Should Know About the RCIA
Charlene Altemose, MSC
#68015 • $4.95

What You Should Know About the "End Times"
Fr. Seán Wales
#67945 • $4.95

Order from your local bookstore or write to:
Liguori Publications
One Liguori Drive, Liguori, MO 63057-9999
Please add 15% ($3.50 minimum, $15 maximum)
to your total for shipping and handling.
For faster service, call toll-free 1-800-325-9521.
Please have your credit card handy.